Hooray!
Jesus is risen

A STORY OF EASTER

BEAUTY IN BOOKS

Hooray! Jesus is risen:

A Story of Easter

ISBN: 978-1-961634-46-6

In a vibrant and colorful town, a group of curious children gathered at the town square, eager to learn about the true meaning of Easter.

Grandma Grace, a kind and wise storyteller, stepped forward to share a tale that would fill their hearts with joy, and hope.

"Children, have you ever wondered why Easter is a time of celebration?" Grandma Grace asked, her eyes twinkling with anticipation.

Wide-eyed and curious, the children nodded in unison. They had heard about colorful eggs and fluffy bunnies, but the true meaning of Easter remained a mystery to them.

"Let me tell you a story that happened long ago,"

Grandma Grace began.

"It's a story of love, sacrifice, and the incredible joy that comes with the Easter message."

Grandma Grace transported the children to a time when the sunlit streets of Jerusalem were filled with excitement. There were whispers of a man named Jesus, who taught about love and kindness.

"Jesus was a very special person who performed miracles and shared stories of hope and compassion," Grandma Grace explained.

"But there were some who didn't understand his message, and he faced many challenges."

The children listened intently as Grandma Grace described in detail how Jesus, filled with love, made a great sacrifice to show that love could overcome anything.

She told them about the cross, the symbol of this sacrifice, and the sadness that filled the hearts of Jesus' friends.

"But here's the most beautiful part," Grandma Grace continued with a warm smile.

"After three days, something miraculous happened.

Jesus rose from the dead!

He defeated sadness and brought hope and joy to everyone who believed in him."

The children's faces lit up with joy and wonder as Grandma Grace painted a vivid picture of Easter morning, with the rising sun shining with a warm glow on a world filled with newfound hope.

Grandma Grace looked at the children with a twinkle in her eye, and said, "Children, Easter is a time to celebrate the victory of love over sadness, hope over despair.

Jesus showed us that love and kindness can bring joy even in the toughest times. Just like Jesus, let Easter remind you to always spread love, kindness, and joy to everyone around you, and make the world brighter."

And with that, the children left the town square with hearts full of Easter joy, and a newfound understanding of the season's true meaning.

The End

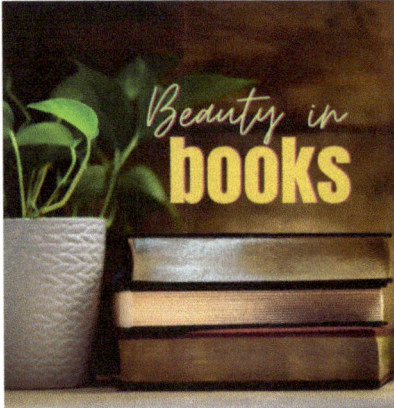

About the Author

"Abyy Sparklewood is an accomplished author with a unique talent for crafting captivating children's fiction and insightful business books. With a playful imagination and a keen business sense, her stories ignite young minds and inspire entrepreneurs to reach new heights of success."

Check out my other books by
Scanning the QR code or using
the link below

linktr.ee/beautyinbooks3